low self-esteem

suicidal thoughts

broken heart

pride

doubt

depression

self-sabotage

SIMONE ALAKEE

low self-esteem

suicidal thoughts

broken heart

pride

doubt

depression

self-sabotage

not my mama's faith

GOD'S MIRACULOUS MARVELOUS MIRACLE

BASAR PUBLISHING

Table of Contents

Acknowledgements

We did it, Jesus!

Thank You God for allowing me to see myself the way You see me. I know that I am not the best daughter always, but Your grace, mercy, favor and presence have never left me.

To the Holy Spirit- Thank You for holding me close.

To my mentor, sister, and book midwife Rekesha Pittman, I am forever grateful that you prayed with me and remained when no one else would.

To my many friends, associates and family, There are so many of you to thank! I want you all know that you are loved greatly by the LoveBug for life and there is nothing you can do about it.

To Tara, you met me at the stoplight. Thank you for the lessons taught even when I was not willing to learn.

To my brother, Dexter, you believed in me when I did not want to believe in myself. For that I am grateful.

To Natalie, the best roommate in the world, we are still going strong and I can now give you some socks!

To my Parents, near, far and resting in a better place, I love you and thank you for the many lessons taught, learned and experienced.

To the elders, first ladies and pastors who have prayed for me, visited with me and encouraged me, I love you and thank you forever.

To my sorors, thank you for always being true Doves in my life. You all will forever be So Sweet.

To my three Mothers, I love you all—each one for different reasons, but simply because you love me. I am a better woman because of you all.

Mama Theresa, I would not have made it out of Mississippi without you.

Mama Wendy, I have survived Las Vegas because of you.

Mommy, without you praying and giving me back to God, I certainly would not have made it this far. We are still together!

Introduction

This book was birthed from a series of events over a span of 10 years, from 2005 up to this great year of celebration 2015. I did not know then that it would be used as a testimony now but then again that is just how God does things, in his own unique way.

I am still on this journey towards my destiny and purpose so, I do not proclaim to be better than anyone because I know God; nope, that is not me at all. I am just ready to be transparent and help someone along the way.

May the words in this book be encouraging and uplifting.

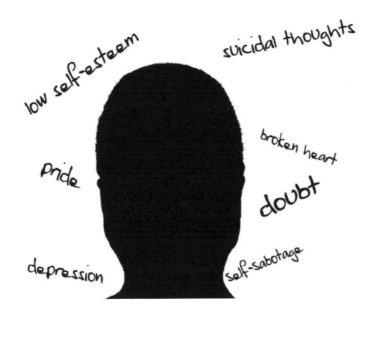

Chapter 1

Here We Go

"Are you ready? We will not be late for church!" This is the one phrase that I can recall hearing on any given Sunday at 7:00 a.m. "Why so early?" I asked and often asked aloud. "Since God made us, sees us and knows us, can't He just accept my fellowship from last week and keep it moving?"Of course there was never a verbal reply; just that typical look that only a praying mother can give.

So I went to church, sang the songs, read the Scriptures and had communion. I even had cake sometimes too, but did it have to be every single Sunday? I really did not understand this at all.

I started to like it a little bit more when I realized that I had a gift to sing. I then wanted to attend every service I could, especially during the week, but I at least wanted the weekends off. Mom would always tuck me in at night by reading a Scripture and saying a prayer. I would wait until the end and ask God, "Lord, may I have a pass for this Sunday?" Mom would then kiss my forehead and say, "Lord, I give her back to you, keep my baby."

What did she mean by that, *keep her baby*? Was she going to leave or was she about to go to work for a long time? Why was she asking God to keep me? Was I becoming a burden to my mama already? I remember sitting at the table for dinner asking mama one day, "What do you mean when you ask God to keep your baby?" She laughed and said calmly, "One day you and God will have to have your own relationship, but until then you are with me and God."

Well, now I am 35 and God knows I have gone through many fires only to come out as pure gold. I am able to say with a bold spirit and happy heart, "I thank God for a praying mother." But just like she said when I was younger, God and I would have to have our own relationship. At this point of my journey, we have that and then some. God and I have always had a connection; it just had to flourish and grow into the rose of trust and form the stable foundation that it has today.

A few things must be explained in order for you to really understand the reason behind the message. This book is written to encourage and inspire. There will be some page-turning moments and also tear-dropping situations, but please give God all the glory because I lived to tell my story and help someone along the way.

Whew! Now that all the formalities are out of the way and proper disclosures are done, let us now travel down just a few of the roads that were once blocked off, rerouted for construction, and simply promised to myself to never be traveled upon ever again. This is what I call looking back to see how far I've come and then realizing that I am one of God's miraculous marvelous miracles. God gets all the glory for sure!

As I stated before, some of these moments will be page-turning, but then again, were not some in the Bible as well? I mean, if God had not allowed some of the chosen to endure what they endured they would have never known how strong their faith was or how important a relationship with God is for that matter. That statement alone deserves a praise break ! if you would like to, go ahead do so, *but* we have a lot to discuss! Pass the collection plate.

Since you have gotten a praise break in and we are bonding, let me prepare you for this journey. I've heard it said, in all things get an understanding (Proverbs 4:7); therefore, you must realize the importance of being transparent with the ability to be questioned with either words, looks or flat out judgment. I must say, I had to press through a lot of resistance. I was not at all open to taking you on this look back. I heard a wise man once say that **we become so others can become,** therefore it is not about me anyway. It is about someone being able to look at any obstacle in the face and say boldly, "You may have caused me to bend, but I did not break!"

Roads Traveled

In order to fully understand why I love music and why I really try to find a melody in everything, we— yes, you and me—are going to have to visit some of

3

the roads I traveled willingly, unwillingly and simply just because something or someone looked interesting. Just before we get to that, let me make this clear: laughter is also a part of God's plan. If you are unsure that God had a sense of humor, just look at some of the names in the Bible, e.g., Bathsheba... Need I explain more?

There is a song that is sung in, you know, that "secular world" that talks about boots and what they are made for. Friend, if they would have given me a pair to walk in while on some of these different boulevards, avenues, lanes and the streets that run on forever, then maybe I would have remembered them better and not walked on them again and again, (and did I mention again?). But God did promise rest to all those who are heavy laden. I guess I wanted to make sure I got it all. Now, if you are coming with me you must pray with me too, okay? Pass me my water bottle, this particular road here is a dusty one.

The Boulevards

The boulevards were the roads that I thought ran on forever and ever. These were the roads (courses, pathways, tracks) in my life that I wish I had placed a permanent roadblock in front of, but in reality, as I reflect, if I had never gone down these numerous boulevards I would never have known or seen my strength.

4

The boulevards have had major beautification projects done on them. There have been days when nothing could pass because there was a lot of tarring going on. I already know the question you are about to ask; *how can one be tarred on a boulevard?* It is all a part of the process. In order for a road to be smooth and easy to drive on, it must be stripped of all the bumps and uneven cement and then done over.

When this was happening I did not get it. I had just graduated from college and returned back to my home city of San Francisco. I just knew this was a mistake. When the headaches began to arrive, I just ignored them and kept skipping down this boulevard of beautification. Come to think of it, that is the name we shall call it: **Beautification Boulevard**. This is the only "road" that I am happy to say I am glad that I visit every now and then. It is here where I am able to really hear from God. I will come back to this road. I am so glad you are with me.

I love God more and more! Seeing the Scriptures come alive in your life is awesome. It is written that to everything there is a season and this is our season to bond and grow (Ecclesiastes 3:1). Now let me get you some water and some tissue; you are going to need all of that and more as we continue.

The avenues are the streets that are short, quick and to the point. The **Avenues** consist of **Doubt**, **Pride**, **Depression** and **Low-Self Esteem**. The one common factor they share is that they leave some pretty heavy stains.

I know when we wash clothes we have products such as Shout—or some sort of stain remover—and as individuals we have our tears. However, there are some stains sometimes that even our tears and stain removers cannot remove. This is why the blood of Jesus is the best and only stain remover I ever want to use. It will lift all dirt and residue and leave no trace at all.

I mean, look at you and I. We do not even look like anything we have been through. It is not because of products, it is because of the blood of Jesus. I know this is going to lead to a praise break, so I am going to have to pull over with you and get my praise in on the side of the road. I too, know how good God is.

If it had not been for God on this journey with me, I would not be able to take this trip with you and help you see that there is a light in and at the end of the hallway. It may be a long hallway or a huge field, but on the other side there is joy, peace and favor. God answers yes and amen (2 Corinthians 1:20).

I can always remember hearing my mother say, "Keep living baby, you will understand all of this one day for yourself." Well, here I am at my 10-year anniversary of what medicine and science said should have been the end, but God said, "I have more for you and I give you beauty for ashes."

Shall we continue, friend? Do you think you can handle more of this journey? Let me know. I do want you to continue with me, but if you need to continue praising God, then lie down, and I'll go get you a shawl.

Okay, now I am turning this corner slowly because I really did not want to come down this road, but I have to in order to go forward. This is not about me but it will help someone else. This is the **Masking Lane**. Water, please with every cup of wine —I mean grape juice—you can find. Bring bread, too. I need communion, the two fish (preferably tilapia) and make it 10 loaves of bread. We need to eat while we travel. Okay... now we will be covered the rest of the way.

This is tough but so necessary. **Self-sabotage** or **Masking Lane** as I call it, did not occur until I got off the **Avenues** and began to wander. See, this is why it is good for us to fellowship together. The church is already in you and you gather to encourage—not to judge, out-dress or gossip about one another. You never know what someone may be going through, dealing with, running from—or, better yet—in need of.

Let me elaborate on what masking is. Masking is pretending with great cover-ups and add-ons. Just like a woman can add lashes, one can add a smile when they really want to cry. He or she can mask all hurt until the lights and people are away. This is where I saw the Scripture that talks about **Pride** coming before a fall (Proverbs 16:18).

I had gotten frustrated and irritated with my mother because all things that were once promised to me were nowhere to be found. I felt like I was owed an explanation as to why this happened when I did what I was supposed to do. I did not trust anyone and decided that I wanted get away and begin somewhere where no one knew me at all—Las Vegas—the dry, hot desert. What was I thinking? Just because I vacationed here should not have meant that I wanted to live here, but I was a fresh college graduate who believed someone owed me something.

I get to my new city and there was still a blessing waiting for me. I was able to transfer with my job and open a major anchor store on the infamous Las Vegas Strip. I was able to keep my medical insurance, get a steady paycheck and yet, I still walked around aimlessly on this tight **Masking Lane**.

You would think I would get it or catch on some kind of way due to me having a headache every single day. Eventually, I had to ask a co-worker to walk with me up and down the stairs at the age of 24. No, not me! I had to appear to like I had all things together.

Even when my family came to visit and see my new place, I never mentioned to them that I was not sleeping at all and that I could not see them half the time. I was the princess and I had a reputation to maintain, so I thought. I soon learned that, yes, I am a princess, but not of the world. I am the daughter of God and because He is my Father and King, I want the things He has promised me.

I wandered in this lane far too long. God had to get my undivided attention to make sure I would no longer run, question or even think I was owed anything from anyone besides respect. I finally asked my mother to go with me to my appointment and see what was going on with my head. What was causing all these headaches? Thank God she did. I was not prepared for all of what would happen next, but again, to everything there is a season and a reason.

This is a great place to stop and exhale. I have to keep emphasizing the importance of reflection. When you go from remembering everything to only being able to remember something by a picture or hearing a song, you too would appreciate and enjoy what you could recall in detail. It is because of my brain surgeries—5 to be exact—that my memory has been challenged. I like to say that God allows me to remember what is necessary, like my name, address and the style and class of the diamond my assigned Boaz must have.

I will always remember this particular doctor's visit like it happened yesterday. I had an appointment with my neurologist and I had it understood that we were going to go over my symptoms and go from there. If only it had happened that way... Once the doctor entered the room, I felt a bit nervous. It reminded me of the days with my father who was a diabetic, amputee, very sickly and always in and out of some doctor's office. The only thought that ran through my mind at that time was, *"Oh no, not me too! I promised mama I would not put her through this. "*

As I had hoped, the doctor heard me out and said that x-rays were needed in order to proceed. I got happy for a moment because I just knew I was going to leave... but this is Las Vegas and this good doctor happened to be right across from the hospital. So I left, only to walk over an overpass to an ER and wait for an x-ray.

Why God? Why? What do you want from me? I give and give and give and give and dare I say it again, give, and now I have to wait for an x-ray? Okay, fine. I will wait, but I am not happy about it.

Have I told you how happy I am that you are here with me on this necessary recap of how good God has been and will continue to be to you and me as long as we keep our faith in Him and Him alone? I know I need to explain to you what happened at the ER, but praise breaks are necessary and in order along this recap.

I had the x-ray done and the technician came back only to look at my mother and I and give us a message that we must go right back to the doctor's office immediately. Look, we can go... but can a girl get something to drink and eat, please? Since we are on the topic of my needs, pass me my makeup bag, I must always be a lady.

Back to the doctor's office we go, and as they say in forms of production, "Lights, camera and action!" I just knew this was a movie for real. I mean it had to be, right? There was no way that I was a college graduate and now about to embark on this journey of faith and humility. I had just turned 25 and was at a place in my life where I knew I could only go up from here. This is where I should have run to any open altar and just lay out or ask someone to pinch me...I just knew that this was not happening to me!

My mother and I had been sitting in the waiting room of the doctor's office for about 20 minutes when the nurse called me and asked that I first come back by myself. I remember saying to her, "No, thank you. I need my mama. This day has been crazy enough." She brushed my shoulder and whispered, "I can imagine," and signaled my mama to accompany me.

Once we got to the room, the doctor was sitting there reviewing the x-rays and shaking his head. I said, "Hello again," and he turned around and asked me if I was one who believed in God. You should know by now that I love God and there is no question about it, but when a doctor asks you that at the beginning of what should have been a regular visit, even the most saved person is a bit nervous. If they say that they are not, just tell them I said, "Keep living and believing."

I looked at my mom and grabbed her hand quickly. The doctor then asked me to sit down so he could go over my x-rays with me and discuss the next plan of action. I sat up in the chair, looked over at my mom and said to the doctor, "Let's just get to the x-rays. What is going on and why is this so important?"

The doctor then said to me, "Simone you have a massive tumor on your brain that must be removed and your diagnosis is Arnold Chiari Malformation, or in simpler terms, pseudo tumor cerebri."

What, what does this all mean? A tumor... a malformation... a what? I am hearing him, but I do not understand any of the words that are coming out of his mouth. All I am able to do is look at my mama who is sitting with me, holding my hand, shaking her legs, and humming a song.

"Wait, wait, wait! Can you please explain this again in simple terms?" He said, "You have a brain tumor and your blood vessels are very small but when you have a headache your brain swells and the excess fluid has nowhere to go; this is why you are having so many headaches and seizures." I then replied, "Okay, so this does cause for surgery and if it does, it is only one correct?"

Just like you paused and went back to read that explanation again in silence, that was how still the atmosphere was in the room. You felt the *worry mechanics* in everyone's mind moving and beginning to form all the questions. The when, what, where, why, how and who were already forming in my mind. What challenges I would now face and how long I would be down? I just wanted to get it over with so I could go on with my life. My mama had questions, but for the first time she was very quiet. This should have been a sign for me, but in reality I was trying to just get to the next page of my new chapter of 25.

"Okay, okay, okay! What needs to happen?" These words were coming out of my mouth with a great tremble in my voice. My body was shaking, along with my faith for the first time, too. "I remember it like it was yesterday" might be an overused cliché, but when you experience one of life's unpaved boulevards you have a new respect for the quotes that are overused, or in this case, not used enough.

The doctor looked at me and asked me if he could have his partner come in and discuss the options with mama and me. All I could do was nod my head in agreement and look at my mother. Her head was down, legs shaking, she was rubbing her hands together. "What does this mean?" I asked her, "What does all this mean?" The doctors were present. One sat in front of me while the other stood behind my mother. One opened with a joke by saying, "Simone, your mother says that your head is big because you hold a lot of knowledge in there. Is that true?" I did not laugh. I just said, "Yeah okay, what is going on?" The head neurosurgeon then said, "You need to have brain surgery due to the fact that you have a tumor on your brain that needs to be removed."

Did he just tell me that I need brain surgery? My life then flashed before me quickly. I saw myself as a baby, a child, a teen and the woman I was to be. I saw the mouth of my doctor moving but heard nothing coming out.

My life was about to be rattled and shaken forever. What am I going to do? Is this the situation my mother was talking about where I would have to lean and depend on God and God alone? This was the part of the journey where it was not my mama's faith that carried me. It was now time for my relationship with God to be on the front line, tested and tried. As I'd often heard the elders say, "If you are going to talk the talk, then you'd better walk the walk, too!" My question was, "Could I endure all of this?"

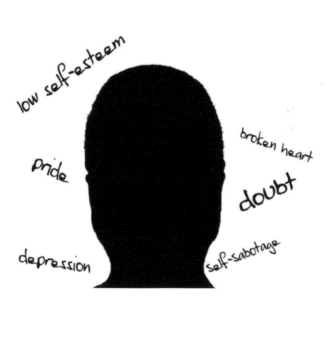

Chapter 2

My Second Birthday

January 26, 2005 will always hold a special spot in my heart; it is my second birthday. Now... do not look at me like that! I told you that I am the princess and because I am royalty, there are just a few things that need no explanation. This day will forever be remembered as the first day of this new journey; **Simone's Own Walk of Faith**.

I was taken down for surgery. Mama had just given me a kiss and said a prayer with me. My soul sister was there (who had also made sure my haircut was gorgeous) and I had spoken to many angels and prayer warriors the night before. I was ready, besides, I really wanted the anesthesia because it was cold. I had a headache, as usual. I was a bit nervous but I remembered that I had sought spiritual counsel from the elders, church friends and my family. I was covered, prayed up and ready.

Once we actually arrived to the waiting area for surgery, mama came back once again. She looked at me with no tears at all and said, "You are my ride or die and we are going to get through this together. Who loves you baby?" I laughed and told her, "You do, mommy and God loves us both. I am ready and cold." We both laughed and then the nurses and surgery crew (as I like to call them) came and took me back to the operating room. As we made our way back there, I heard a nurse say to me, "I like your pedicure." I said to her, "Thank you," but even a princess can be nervous *and* cute, right? She laughed and promised me that I would be okay and not to worry. I took one last sigh, looked up and began to count with the doctor...one, two, sleep.

When I finally awakened from surgery, I had the joy of hearing my mama humming the Winnie the Pooh theme song in my ear. Yes, some time had passed from the day of my surgery and when I finally became responsive. I was monitored daily, but it was not until I heard my mama humming the Winnie the Pooh song in my ear, that I became responsive. I looked up at her and said, "Hey, mommy. Is my lipstick on? Did you pay my rent? Are my feet still cute?" She yelled with gratitude, "Thank You, Jesus! My baby is okay!"

I know the response was different, but I have a few close people in my life hexagon who will probably chuckle when they read that particular part simply because they know me. Yep, I was back and all systems were good. Well... not completely good, but I was coherent enough to come off one of the three machines I was connected to.

The nurses and doctors came running into my room asking me a million questions and checking every vital sign that a human being needed to have checked. I believe this is why I do not like needles, thermometers or blood pressure cuffs to this day.

When a person has been in a coma and they finally become responsive, allow them some time to gather themselves together and then check their vitals. Everybody is not saved or a part of the blood washed crew. They may possibly slap you back to your mother, or close to it! Everybody remembers Peter, right?

I honestly thought that the surgery and coma were enough and—believe me when I say this—God did not have to allow anything else to happen for me to know or understand that He loved me and heard me. When He has a calling for you and only you, God must make sure that you are with Him for the right reasons. I see you trying to understand and I knew you were going to ask me, "What reasons?"

God had given us free will and has already promised us life more abundantly. Yes, He has, but He has to be a fair God and allow you to see both sides of the coin. Since you and I have both grown up in the church (or at least been outside of the building on one of the many nights that there was a revival, shut-in or just a plain meeting), we have heard every Bible story, Vacation Bible School program, and Sunday School lesson. We know about the parting of the Red Sea, how Lazarus was brought back to life, the blind were able to see, and water was turned into wine—which was not at a local wedding down the street but it actually happened while Jesus was here. When He returns, there will again be miracles, signs and wonders. I believe this amazement has come because He chose to deal with someone like me.

When I was younger, I used to take voice lessons. We would always end each rehearsal with "Ordinary People." There is line in the song that says, "Little becomes much when you place it in the Master's hand." This is what had to happen with my life. I had to place my little, tiny, unimportant life (or so I thought), in the hand of God and allow Him to make it much.

Let me remind you that I was 25 years of age when this surgery happened. Remember how I mentioned that I had a memory before that could retain everything? Well, I had good motor skills and hand/eye coordination too. However, things do change in life and sometimes what we forget to appreciate the simple things. After being responsive and getting medication for just about every pain, I thought that I was ready to get back to life as I recalled it. **Newsflash:** If you need to ask for help, do so. It is when you do not you truly end up hurting yourself.

I made that note because after that surgery, I went from being a recent college graduate to being a 25 year old young woman who had to go through excessive rehabilitation for the simple things in life. I had to walk with assistance, eat with assistance and do a lot, if not all, of the independent things we often take for granted with assistance. I still get excited and often laugh because I really do appreciate hand/eye coordination and the ability to take care of myself in a simple and private way. Now, you know if we were in church that would be a praise break!

My tumor was removed. I was in rehabilitation and I was prepared for the placement of my first shunt. Wait a minute... This was not what was explained initially and I was still trying to grasp the concept of rehabilitation.

Honestly speaking, I heard of rehab but always associated it with drug addicts or alcoholics. Never in my mind would I have ever placed a woman of my caliber in "rehab." Rehabilitation was necessary and needed like forgiveness is needed for all of our sins and shortcomings. I had to be taught the basics all over again, from kindergarten to high school. What? This was not a part of the plan or agreement, Lord! Nevertheless, it was reality. This was the part of the plan that would allow me to spend many, many nights just sitting and crying. I would often cry with or without a pen.

When I had a pen, I would find myself writing out all of my questions or thoughts that were on the tablet of my heart. That amazed me because earlier in the day, I could not say or pronounce anything at all. At night, when the sky was darkest and no one was around, after the nurses had gone home and mama was asleep, was the only time I could speak or write and understand. I did not get it then, but looking back now, I understand that it happened that way in order for me to know for sure that God and I had a definite connection with each other.

There was one particular night that I sat up in my bed at the rehab facility and cried out with a pen. With that pen flowed tears and notes to the melody of my heart that went like this:

Dear God,

It is me once again! I am coming to You the only way I know how; naked, flawed and crying out loud. My heart is sincere and my arms are outstretched. It seems lately my spirit is vexed. You have my attention and my hand; please do not let it go; for without You I will not be able to stand. Keep me in Your arms where it is warm and safe.

For I know it is there that you will keep me for this race.

Lord you know I am scared and really unsure...
God what do I do?

Who can I talk with and feel like a fool?

Why is it that my past seems to always want to hang around?

It's like the devil knows a seed for me was planted long ago on solid ground.

*It will be okay soon, right? I think I do see a light.
It is away in the distance but what is far to me, to
You is near.*

*I do know that You love me, for You have kept me
here.*

*Just let me know every moment in the day that Your
hand is always near.*

*I want to get over this hump in the road, so I am
willing to give You all the load.*

I love You Lord. Thanks for EVERYTHING?

It was during my rehabilitation days that I often
found myself wanting to end each day with a note to
God. I continued to go through the treatments and
testing. When the time came for more surgeries, I
found that I got a little bit stronger and was able to
laugh more, communicate better and feed myself
too. Maybe if I would go back to those days at least
twice a week, the rest of this weight would come off.
Help me, Jesus.

There were more surgeries that followed that
one, but God did not use just the surgeries to get my
attention and keep the connection growing. He used
other life experiences as well. One that really stood
out was my first trip back to my hometown of San
Francisco. I was so excited! It was the first trip after

my second birthday and it was in September; close to my first birthday.

I was traveling on an airplane for the first time since the first makeover. It was different, but as the plane ascended I just told myself that I was flying towards the doors of heaven and not to worry. I know I was okay because I slept until the flight attendant had to come over and wake me up. Resting with God is a good thing, as I have learned.

Once I arrived in the Bay Area, I was able to meet up with family and friends. It was at this moment that I began to notice that my memory was changing. I did become concerned, but like anyone who has taken medication, I blamed it on that. I remember driving by a neighborhood. I was sure that it had changed but my aunt and uncle ensured me that it had not. I looked out the window and found the brightest star; for to me that was the eye of God. As I looked up with concern, I asked God, "Are You sure things have not changed?"

It was when I returned to Las Vegas that I began to make more appointments. At one in particular, mama was present. I informed the doctor that I noticed my memory was changing. I wanted to know why. The doctor looked at me with all sincerity and replied, "It is going to change and something that you once remembered, you may recall differently or simply not at all." What? Once again, this was not part of my plan for me at all. This was not fair and really should not be. Why? Why was this happening to me?

I looked at my mama and shook my head. I was angry, hurt, confused and scared. This was only the icing; the cake itself was that I would have to go through one more surgery.

As if that was not enough, I had a job that I had to now walk away from due to medical issues. I could only work part-time. To top it all off, my father passed away during that time as well.

If there was ever a time that I wanted to just get mad and question God, it was during that season which lasted forever in my eyes. In reality, it was nine years. From 2005 until 2014, I seemed to reside in the hospital. I had a room with a view, without a view, with a roommate, and private too. However many ways you can have a room in a hospital, believe me, I had experienced all of it! I had visitors come and visitors go. While in that season, I kept hearing a consistent, calming voice that would always meet me in my midnight hour—that can sometimes be in the middle of the day. I was learning then what it meant to know Jesus for yourself.

There came a time when I just wanted to rebel and do what I wanted to do. Like I said, my season of medicinal obstacles lasted from 2005 to 2014 and it seemed like my mailing address should have been at any hospital in Clark County. On the days that I was at home, stable and free; the rebel in me stepped up to the plate. Remember how I stated that God has a sense of humor? I know for sure He does because of the situations He allowed me to get myself in. I truly had a desert experience, not the kind where you may see one yearning for water in the physical form, but the kind of experience where God would be the only person, place and thing that could and would carry me up, over and out of all situations.

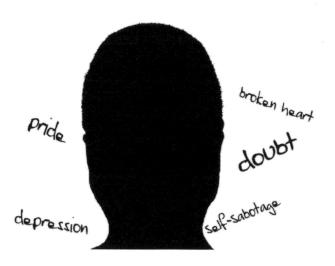

Chapter 3

The Desert Experience

I wanted to move to Las Vegas because I wanted to begin again and be grown. Little did I know that just because you are of a certain age does not mean that you are grown or ready to handle all of life's curve balls that are either thrown at you or by you. There were several moments that I found myself acting like a girl when I should have been a woman or allowing my mouth and the words that came from it to get me in situations that I knew for sure were not part of my moral fiber or character period.

Oh Lord… I have been talking, laughing out loud and shaking my head. I hope you are still with me, friend? I do not want to scare you at all or receive empathy or sympathy. I just want you to know that no matter what you do, where you go or how you behave; when God loves you He loves you. If you are one of the few who are chosen, just stay ready and humble. The roads are never easy, but the peace, grace, mercy and favor are priceless. You still with me? This part of the journey is funny; keep reading.

It is here in this desert that I wanted to be my own grown person. I wanted to be liked, have friends, go partying and only seek the fellowship of church when I felt I needed to. I figured since I had gone to church so much as a child, I should get a pass as an adult. Besides, I am in a city whose nickname is "Sin City." Jesus paid it all so I can sneak away and do what I want.

Whew, Lord! Thank You for loving the sinner. Friend, oh friend... If only I had paid close attention to the woman at the well or the woman with the issue of blood or even the many women of the night who God later used for His glory, this story would not be told in this manner. But then we would not have this time to grow together. I am glad I know for sure now the importance of my walk and with whom I talk. It has been said by a songwriter and many pastors that we become so that others can become. Let me just make one nice request; please take all the notes you can and ask me anything. As my mama would say, don't you let my prayers or experiences have been in vain.

I had brought baggage with me that should have been dropped off, thrown out and simply left alone. I had feelings from the many roads traveled because I kept traveling down the road over and over again. I wanted the approval of man so much that I was willing to give all I had just to have companionship (so I thought). I was so lost that I would leave work, go home, get ready to go out with people and allow them to misuse and abuse me just to fill a avoid that I myself created.

This is how I know that God had His hand on me even when I was teetering on the fence of what is right and acceptable and what is incorrect. I would leave situations with my head down and cry out, "Lord if you can just get me out of this, I will never do it again or again or again." I know you think I should have gotten the picture. Heck, I thought I should have too, but I was enjoying temporary pleasure that could have cost me more permanent pain. I did not know that all of those moments, temper tantrums, harsh words and the desire for approval would have happened in what looked like a barren land. It later turned out to be an oasis; in the valley of a desert where the mountains are peaking and God is present and always near. It was in this experience that I gained a new understanding of how God felt when He is brokenhearted.

I had been looking for love in all the wrong the places. This time, I just knew I had found love in the right place. We were friends that drifted apart but reconnected after what I thought was a relationship ended. There I go again in my emotions and making permanent decisions based on a something not even temporary. Do not turn your head and cough on me now! I have to be honest and transparent.

Here I am; he and I; talking, laughing and so sweetly saying "Hi." Little did I know that this would be the best and last lesson in ignoring the love I have. Because he was away and claimed he wanted to be near, he surprised me with a visit and filled my heart with temporary cheer. We embraced, laughed and even went to capture this whole thing. We took pictures and looked at wedding rings—you read correctly—wedding rings.

How many times does a woman really want to get married? No answer, no problem I will answer for me; one honey only one. So we are looking at rings and he and I are all giddy with things, only to find in the end it was a lie that I wished was a dream. It was something that you read about when you and I were 17. If only I had not been so quick to want to fit in the main scene. Wait... do not make a fist or want to get even on my behalf, I had all the warning signs. Remember how mama always said a hard head makes a soft behind? That was what had happened and the only person that could soothe me or calm me was God.

I felt like this happened to make sure He had my attention. Believe me, He did but there was still a few things I wanted to do. I continued to be angry because I got my heart trampled on and I believed no one was there for me. I was more than wrong. I was another woman living my emotions and feeling like I had to get even—if not with the man who I allowed to hurt me—then with men period.

Now you know that I know that was not the best thing and should not have been an option. Sometimes this is why cycles repeat; we keep ourselves there when the only thing God wants us to do is release all of ourselves to Him. It is in moments like these that we should remember the most remembered Psalm, number 23. This is the one reminds us why we are to trust God. He is our Shepherd, which means He will protect, provide and care for us. That right there just placed a smile on my heart. He loves us, you and me so much that He will provide all that we need. No matter what it may be, we must trust in Him and Him alone.

I found myself gathering my thoughts again, pen and paper in hand, only to sit down and look out at a tree and write these simple words:

Wow, reality has hit
Happiness keeps you sweet, trials keep you strong
Sorrow keeps you human, failures keep you humble
Success keeps you glowing; only God keeps you going
Make it a great day, the sun is shining
Good days give you happiness; bad days give you
experience
Is this why I have forced my bad days to outweigh my
good days?

I did not understand what my heart was saying then but as I am writing this I realize more that God never left me, I wandered away from Him.

There were many more incidents that happened along this journey. If you ask me, all of them stand out, but you know when you take the time to reflect back on the roads you have traveled you see that there are just a few in each chapter that stand out. This is not done in order from beginning to end; this is just my recollection and the few of many reasons why I love God, life and love. I believe that some-times when you talk things out, it helps you to get a better understanding as to why things happened the way they did. Now, I did not say that I enjoyed look-ing back, but if my mistakes can help you avoid a few mistakes, then let's continue to look back and re-joice.

Speaking of rejoicing, did I tell you how I left the desert only to come right back and love it even more? This is how it went: I wanted to get away from Las Vegas because I was still "mad" with my decisions, some of which I had on repeat. I thought going to a big state such as Texas would be good. Oh it was good alright; it made me miss and once again go through yet another form of rehabilitation. Get this part of the message at least, please; a burn is a burn no matter how you are burned, okay?

I get to the great city of San Antonio only to have another knock at my heart. From Who? The Man Himself. I had plans, but when God has a plan for you, please trust it. You may want to be in a big house because you feel you deserve that but God will have you to take refuge with people who start off as strangers but end up being all a part of the set up.

I had the pleasure of attending a blessed church only to have my own Naomi and Ruth experience. Can you believe it? Me, having this type of moment. Though it is not in the desert itself, it too was a part of the desert experience.

My Naomi happened to be a woman who was from Las Vegas. She was so beautiful, a wife, mother and now my first midwife. We met at church and from there we had a bond that I now know and realize even more was ordained and is maintained by God alone. She reached out to me and I thought I had cracked the door of my heart, to later realize that I had completely opened my heart to her. It is written in the scriptures that we are to confess our sins one to another. I now understand why, when you speak aloud the things that you have done or may even want to do that you know goes against God to someone who has a real every day, every situation relationship with Him, it allows you to begin to see the scriptures come to life.

I now had my own Naomi and she had a lot to share with me. Being that I was Ruth, I worked. I had a part time job that would allow me to meet some-one new every day. It was during this experience that I was able to begin to take notice of all of God's creatures. This may make you laugh but I respect all animals. This includes any that can donate hair, walk a person to and from a corner and sing you a song. Have you figured out which two I am speaking of? Let me help you, a horse and a beautiful bird. Yes, I had a horse that would meet me at the corner to go to my job and the bird would sing me a song every morning to awaken me. I began to see during this ordained moment the importance of prayer and worship.

I would often ask my Naomi, why is God allowing me to endure this time and have to begin again? She laughed one day and said to me, "Because you must begin to appreciate all that you have and all that you will endure." I did not get that then but talking about it with you now, I can truly say that I appreciate all things experienced. I believe that this was said to me right before I made a return to Las Vegas. Do you know that even to this day we still communicate and pray for each other? It is because of that experience that I was able to sit down and write this about God one night:

Completeness
One can never really have it without Me
I am the Alpha and Omega and all things in between
Yet you feel the need to attempt some if not all things without Me
Haven't you realized that I blocked your path, created your delays?
I have been waiting to hear your heart say
I need You Lord, I need You
But instead you try because of pride to make it all the way through
I must admit that my heart aches because I love you so much but yet
I haven't earned your unconditional trust?
It's okay My child, I will still be here with open arms and immeasurable forgiveness

I hope you return before I do, for all I ever want to do is

COMPLETELY
COMPLETE
YOU.

I have been back in Las Vegas for about 12 days now and it has honestly been more difficult this time. See right now, I am here in this city by myself. My mother had to depart in order to handle her affairs. That is good though, because I am grown and ready to handle whatever comes my way. I may have thought that but in reality I was not ready to handle anything.

I found myself going to casinos and spending money that I know I had no business spending. I was enjoying the lights and the wrong attention. Now do not judge me, but I told you I was going to be transparent and honest. Just because people do not walk around with a sign on their head that reads "**I have a problem**" does not mean that they do not exist. Remember how I mentioned to you the masks that people wear? I know about them because I have worn many. Yes, worn! Past tense!

In order for me to help the next person I had to remove the mask, seek genuine forgiveness from God, forgive myself for what I did, said and thought to myself and about myself. We will address that in the next segment. The biggest sign of growth was when I was able to forgive anyone who has hurt me. I laugh at it now because when I offer a glass of water I really do mean it. By the way, would you care for a glass too, or would you like some tea or lemonade?

Did you know that when you do not forgive you are adding more weight to your body? I thought it was because of those good old sweet potatoes. You mean to tell me that I could not get in that dress because I did not forgive someone? Okay, from this day forward all are forgiven. Please forgive me and now pass me my dress again; it is too cute to just sit on a hanger in my closet. Honey, you know a princess must always look her best. From that moment on I began to say, "It's cool, no problem," and smile.

Back to one of the **mask** I was wearing: **Gambling**. I knew that it was the wrong thing to do but I was addicted to the idea that I could win some fast money. I mean, I am in Las Vegas and millions are available to win, right? Wrong, wrong, wrong. Las Vegas has truly been the foundation of this entire walk of faith. The excuse I gave myself for gambling was because I wanted to be able to shop freely and get nice accessories for the apartment. I wanted it right then and there but I needed to be patient and allow things to work.

It was like I had forgotten my experience in San Antonio. I had become of those "only talk to God when needed" people. It was when I had gotten myself into a perplexing situation that I prayed. I never claimed to be a perfect saint but I am willing to go back and reveal the moments that caused me to be where I am today, in love and on the same page as God.

I knew that I did not want all that I just endured be in vain but sometimes you really must fall seven times to realize that it is only God who is keeping you through it all. One of the many "in need" prayers I prayed went like this:

"Please forgive me of all my sins and shortcomings. Help me to be that light that I was created to be and guide my thoughts and my words. I love You and need You now more than ever before. I need Your guidance in my finances. You see my situation and my needs. Lord please open the window of heaven that pours right into my bank account and allow me to get out of debt and began anew.

I know that half the battle is that I have not read my word the way I need to and for that I can truly feel and see the difference. I am not going backwards for anyone, not even myself. I am in another chapter of my life, "Chapter 27: Doing all things God's way…" Yep, that is it. I am really excited about that because I think I finally got it. I did not have to lose everything to get it or turn 30 or catch a disease to realize that my body, mind and soul are truly Yours and wherever I go or take it matters.

I am so grateful for this time this morning. I knew that I needed to get up and chat with You first Lord. I love You and thank You for allowing me to have a direct connection to You. Thank You for all that You have done, what You are about to do, and what is to come."

I am so glad that God sees us for who we are. I often remember before my mother was even aware of me, God knew me first. It sounded good and sincere but even my left pinky toe knew it was not from my heart. When you truly seek forgiveness from God, there is a feeling that comes over you that feels like a burden has be lifted and you find yourself not even pondering on those things anymore. I did get that once I became sincere in my prayers and actions. there will be more of that as we look back together.

Now with this return back, seeking quick pleasure from a slot machine brought more and more headaches, which often lead to seizures. I was often mad and questioned all of it. How could I get mad, when I had created most of this? I looked to man to complete the void that was there. I allowed the hurt from a childhood incident to linger and used it as an excuse for my behavior. I thought because one man hurt me, ALL men after had to pay. That was not a smart thing to do or ever act upon. I was the only one who was hurt and feeling less and less of a woman. I had to often look in the mirror and make myself smile. Thank God for tears! They not only cleanse the soul but it allow you see a bit more clearly each time you cry.

There was one particular incident that occurred in this beautiful desert experience. I was at my birthday party and was really feeling myself. The night went on and soon the sun came up. I used to ask, "Why is it that I remember some things and then others I really have forgotten?" This was answered as I pondered this particular incident. My brother had flown into town to celebrate with me. We actually had some words that we exchanged in what I like to call a needed reality check. It was not the fact that this was my brother who was telling me about myself, it was that he used one particular phrase that really stuck with me, "If you are going to talk the talk, you need to start walking the walk and stop having a pity party for yourself." WHAT? I never thought that I was having a pity party for myself at all, I just chalked it up to me just living in a possibly rebellious kind of way.

What he said is a cliché that is used by EVERYONE in the church, in the foyer and those waiting to get to the church on the usual CME days; you know what those days are; Christmas, Mother's Day and Easter. I have to honest as we do this looking back together. I was just in awe that he would say that to me at that particular time.

Now that I look back and let you in on this part of the journey, I realize that it was again a set up. If my brother had not sat there and read me my rights and stopped me in my tracks, I know without even guessing to make sure, that I would not be here today. You can say it was at that point that I understood that I have and will continue to walk in my faith and my faith alone.

Now I am not going to go into all the other surgeries that followed after that but I will say that I have a greater appreciation for my journey thus far. You see, the return to the desert was for me to be able to understand why my light must shine. It needs to be bright in all situations. This includes the situations that make no sense to you or the next person but must happen in order to move forward. I had to return the place that I thought was a setup for defeat and dependence on man. I was so wrong.

This desert experience was designed for me to be release from myself, becoming solely dependent on and trusting God. I had to release myself from pride, fear, approval of others and realize that I was here for a reason. I had to realize that asking for help was not a sign of weakness but a sign of maturity. I had to understand that every day will not be perfect but it will have a beautiful song in it somewhere with a lesson attached for me to learn and share. Yes, that was why I had to return to the desert. As a mother of the church said, "I needed to decrease so God would increase."

Chapter 4

A Closer Walk With Thee

So I have now got a better understanding as to why I am here in this Oasis. Now I must begin to form a better relationship with God. I must admit, it was shaky at first. Once again I was provided with some great and experienced angels to help me along the way.

Remember the angel I had in Texas? She and I never lost contact and I would often call her and ask questions. It was on one particular day that I called her and inquired about where and how to begin to build a better relationship with God. She let out what I like to call a big sister sigh because she did not want to laugh to offend me. She said, "You are really too cute." She told me that I needed to just get in a quiet place and begin to talk to Him. She reminded me how much I loved to sing and suggested that I begin with a song from my heart and allow the spirit to flow from there.

Now do not get confused, I knew God. I sang the songs and prayed the prayers that were taught to me and asked to be repeated. It was not until I got back to my Oasis that I realized that this relationship was between Him and I and no one else.

I hung up the phone and grabbed my journal. I sat on the floor of my bedroom and began to write a letter to God. I did not sing a song, I hummed one and began to understand why my mother always said sometimes all you need to do is hum to God and He will understand. I was on the floor and began to rock back and forth as if I was in the arms of my Father; I mean, yes I was. I was in the arms of God and He was sitting there waiting for me to commune with Him.

I knew what was on my mind but my heart had something else to say. I began to write what I now call a letter of concern to God. I found myself being honest and opening up doors of myself that I did not want to open but needed to. There are parts of the letter that I would really like to share with you for one reason. As your sister, I am to encourage you and by doing that I must be willing to be transparent. Aside from that, you have been with me along this look back over my life trip; the least I could do is give you water and the truth.

This part of the letter really moved me because I know it was strictly between God and me. It went like this:

I have concerns that I need to release to you and attain guidance. One concern is my purpose. I never, ever want to experience a deaf ear turned to me. I want to always remain in the favor of You. God, may You please keep me surrounded by all the angels and in good health? I speak to my body, heart, mind, and soul right now; letting them know that God is the source of my life and strength. I am one with You. Another concern is my body and mouth. Lord, I have said some bad things that I know did not water the soul of someone else but there is no excuse. All I can do is seek forgiveness and count to 10. My body in not my own and I cannot be "holy" one day and then be a loose woman another day. That just does not go together. You are the reason why I am still here and disease-free. I am going to make it in this Oasis and be able to tell my story one day.

Now that was a lot to share, but I had to share that to remind you that there will be a breaking point or you will be forced into one. That point will cause you to be still and quiet. Honestly, I would rather have that moment occur willingly than for God to have to get my undivided attention.

I am not even going to sit here and act like after that moment all things got easy and the rainbow shined all day and every day. No, no , no! It got a bit more intense. I began to get talked about, looked down upon and faced more surgery. I thought that I had left all of the desire to be accepted alone. I thought that my mouth was going to improve without any effort and therefore everything that could get to me did. I even relapsed and began to think negatively more and more. I allowed the devil of suicide to enter one more time. I allowed people's opinion to weigh so heavy on me that I would go broke just to make sure I was liked and noticed.

I remember I wanted to fit in so bad with people that I would sit in meetings and smile when in reality I did not want to be there at all. I would just attend because someone I thought was important or a "friend" was going to be there and they needed to see me.

I was more afraid than ever. I was ready or as willing as I thought I was to have a closer walk with God. There were some things that I could not shake off. My question now was, "Why?" I know God heard me because that night on the floor I did not write that letter... it was my spirit but my actions did not line up with those words. Did I lie to God and was I pretending now?

The mask of being **Brokenhearted** should have been the one that just broke me and forced me to surrender all. As you can probably guess, that was not the one that did it. This mask was the one that helped me to understand the difference between a person's words and actions. Now I know you know that infamous thought of your words and actions need to match, but there are some who just like to talk to talk. Having a broken heart is something that the greatest lesson reminds us of: How God's love can truly keep you.

I can see that you are waiting to hear about the experience so I will give you the short version. Like I mentioned before, I was engaged at one point. Yes

Lord—engaged. I had the ring, card and proposal to prove it. What really happened was, I got played, lied to and was left to pick myself up and keep moving.

I found myself so hurt and confused until I did not speak to anyone at all. My mother would come by my apartment and check on me but I would stay in my room and cry. I cried because I was hurt. I cried because I was now angry. I was crying because I wanted revenge.

There was a release from this mask on one particular day; it happened as I was listening to a nice song that spoke to my future days and encouraged me to remember that the best is yet to come. I was listening to that and watching a wonderful movie. I found myself laughing so hard and so much until tears began to flow. I looked up and asked God if this was funny to Him and if it was could He please cease the jokes. At that moment He had my undivided attention.

After that particular moment of cleansing, I got up and pulled out my tablet and began to write. I looked out the window and saw a ray of light that I had never seen before. It looked like a hand was coming towards me. I began to smile a little bit more and then these words came to me:

What do our eyes say?
If eyes are the window to my soul
And the truth You are to see,

Then tell me, what?
What do You see when You look at me?
Do You see my innocence?
Do You see my scars?
Do You see my fears?
Do You see my tears?
Do You see my today with You?
Look, look at me.
Do You see my hopes, my dreams?
Do You see my desire to love?
To love life, to love You...
Do You see all of me from beginning to end?
Look at me; tell me if it is our destiny You see
For these are a few of the things I see
When I look straight into the eyes of Thee!

These were words that spoke to my heart and help-ed me to understand why I saw the hand in the light. God wanted me to release myself into His hands.

God speaks to everyone differently. Some may get a word through a commercial. Another may get it from a person on the bus, or like it happened one day for me in a simple ray of light. Yes, there was a song too, but the ray of light is what really spoke the loudest. Now I understand why it is good to have either the third eye or ear. I mean you may just be one of God's special and favored children and need two of the third eyes—which in simple terms are glasses. Now you understand why I keep my glasses and sunglasses clean.

Having a closer walk with God was long overdue. All the things that had happened to this point, as I look back; were all to get me to a solid stand in my faith.

As you know, masks are worn to cover up one's emotions and true self. They place a cover over your true feelings and keep the essence of who you are hidden. Now what I am saying here is so important— when you put your cover on daily, you begin to believe what you have put on instead of seeing yourself through the eyes of the One who loves you and has loved you through it all.

I have learned that is not fair or necessary for those who are ordained or assigned to be in your life or give you a message. I must make this point after the mask being released because the removal of being **Brokenhearted** allowed me to reveal my true self and take off other masks that I had worn.

Doubt, Self Sabotage, Suicidal Thoughts, Pride, Depression and **Low Self-Esteem** were the masks that were revealed and needed to come off indefinitely. You would think that every time I took off my makeup I would wash off the residue of the masks, but you know me. I thought I had to have the best face, lips and eyes and was not about to allow the money I invested in the different lines I purchas-ed go to waste. Do not look at me like you are shocked or in awe! You know I stay at a makeup counter. The difference now is that I stay there to enhance my beauty, not to make the masks pretty.

51

Since we are discussing makeup, pass me my lip balm and water please, I am going to need a lot for this part of the walk. Again, I am so glad that you are with me because sometimes company is needed. Are you ready for this next leg of the journey?

Now the masks of **Doubt, Self-Sabotage and Depression** were all worn as one. They were like layers of a good cake. As women, we are able to hide things very well and often without any primer or concealer. I know you know what I am talking about. This was worn as one because of the layers and levels of depth. Let me explain what I mean. **Doubt** was the first layer because I was not sure or I did not want to believe that there was anyone who wanted to be around me, love me or just be with me. I did not trust my own thoughts.

When I was seeking advice regarding this mask in particular and the emotions it brought with it, some said that it was because of the rocky relationship I had with my father. Others advised that is was be-cause I was remembering being called that one awful name in high school. Side bar: I am all for joking and having fun but when you pick on someone or bully them, remember that it has an effect on them in more of a negative way instead of being the laugh of the class. Some also suggested that it was a phase I was going through. I will admit that all of those ideas made sense but I had reached this point of owning my part in my life. Whew! That in itself was an eye-opening experience in more ways than one.

I was now trying decipher if it was okay for me to place the blame on what I had experienced in my life or was it time for me take responsibility for placing this mask on my face knowing that God had all of this covered. The famous 23rd Psalm was one that I was able to recite in my sleep, at work and on the bus, but I learned quickly that it was not something I believed. It was something that I could recite and recite very well. Public Service Announcement: always pick your words carefully then ask yourself, "Will these words encourage and produce positivity or will these words hurt and resound loudly at the wrong time?"

I thought the only way people would want to be around me was if I purchased something for them, covered a meal or movie, or put it simply, bought their company. That idea alone was the icing on the cake. That thought led up to level of **Self-Sabotage**; this is one I found myself battling with for the longest time. Even though I was letting things go, I would still pick up my blush brush and brush it on. I will explain what I mean by that in a moment.

Self-Sabotage is defined as part of my personality acting in conflict with another part of my personality. Of course that was the intelligent definition, but in simple terms, it is defined as my spirit fighting my flesh. I can dance about this now because I understand now, but then I did not. I did not realize or even want to see that these thoughts were causing me to miss out on many, many blessings. I did not believe that there were people that were really coming into my life because they saw something in me that they could either relate to or they saw something that they liked.

There was this one particular service I went to that I just knew I had left all things at the altar. I felt lighter and found myself smiling at the end of the service. The old cliché that says, "You won't leave here the same way you came," was showing on me and I was happy, or so I thought. I got home, pulled out my journal and began to write some powerful declarations for the New Year that was quickly approaching. As soon as I wrote these declarations, I began to question EVERYTHING that I was writing, had heard and I was even so bold to think. I wrestled with the thought that God did not want to hear anything from me at all.

Now, you know that was a battle like no other! I began to even look around my apartment to see if anyone else was present. Once I realized that it was no one there but me, I froze. I sat on my couch and looked for that light I had seen before but instead I found myself rocking back and forth. How could I even think that God did not want to hear from me? How could I even allow my thoughts to wander off to that place? I know that He loved me, yet I did not feel deserving of His love. It was at that moment that I remembered my mother telling me that when you cannot speak to God you can always moan or wave your hand because He reads the tablet of your heart.

This particular moment reminded me of making a cake, except it was backwards. Instead of me placing the icing on the different layers and going up, I was removing the icing and getting to the foundation. This moment also had allowed to remove another mask; **Depression.** This is one mask that I must admit had been worn for the longest time. I took it off, but later I as you continue to walk with me you will learn that it was a temporary removal. To make it simple, let me just say that I had intertwined it with **Self-Sabotage**; that mask was totally removed as I stated previously, but **Depression** was one that had extended an extensive stay. I had been overly-concerned about being liked, understood and wanted, that I would allow myself to believe the negative, dishonest words that many would use to describe me or in simple conversation.

I can laugh at this now because I am walking tall and strong with someone who loves me unconditionally and only wants to see me finish the race God Himself has assigned for me to finish. Removing this mask this particular time finally allowed me to understand just how powerful words were. It does not matter when you say something, it matters how you say it. I know you that infamous scripture that talks about life and death are in the power of the tongue, well I would like to add that if you allow yourself to focus on the wrong voice life and death can lie in that too. Do not look at me like that. You understand what I mean.

The best example for me to use would be the time after my third craniotomy (surgery of the brain, I was paying attention in human anatomy). I was having lunch at a restaurant here in my God-given Oasis and I received an important phone call. The call was from the one person I allowed to have a permanent spot in my thought world; it was my father. It was during this phone call that the mask should have been removed, burned and never wanted again, but you know how it is when you put on a dress or outfit and it has good fit—you want wear it all day and every day.

My father called me to apologize and made a confession to the years of abuse he put me through. He spoke to my mother first and then spoke to me. His words felt like a sharp knife in my heart because he said, "I love you and I am so proud of you. If I could go back and undo all that I have done I would, but please accept my apology." I wanted to respond with words that would allow him to know that I was hurt, in bondage and wanted him to feel my pain but to my own surprise all could say was, "I love you too Daddy and God bless." Why did those words come out when that was not what I wanted to say? I know now that I said that because it was God speaking through me and to me at the same time.

I had allowed the years of abuse to linger and replay in mind like a song. I did not mind the music but it was the wrong station. I allowed the actions and words spoken to me to take permanent residency.

My father passed about 3 days after that phone call. I remember smiling as if my life would now begin and be wonderful. Whoa, was I wrong! I removed the mask for that moment, but when no one was looking, I put it back on. This was when I learned for sure that God sees ALL THINGS. It does not matter if no one is around or I am not in the mirror, I know God sees me.

Depression was like a permanent resident. I may have given it an eviction notice but it just kept returning. I got up in the morning and practiced my smile for the day. You know how we working women do when we are getting ready for work—brush our teeth, comb our hair and apply whatever lipstick we have that will help up to feel good all day, right? Wrong! After practicing my smile and forcing myself to laugh at jokes that really made no sense, I would come home, look at my television and ask why until I fell asleep. This became my routine for years. I had gotten so good at it until I believed that I needed to be placed under specific watch just in case.

This would be a good time for you and me to get some more water because there is a steep hill coming up and we are going to need to be ready to climb it. Take a deep breath and get at least seven good gulps. By doing that we will be completely ready for this climb. See how I did that? Seven gulps, completely ready. As you see, this is the only hill along this look back because once we get to the top we will only go up from there. Just wait… you will see in a moment. Remember, this is not my mama's faith!

The reason behind me wanting to be under specific watch was because I had started believing the voices that I allowed to live rent free in my mind. I allowed the words spoken to me to resound like a bell ringing in a cathedral. It became so bad until **Suicidal Thoughts** began to come to the front. Of course with me having the different medical procedures done, I was given different forms of medication that would allow me to be numb and sleep. Now, do not get me wrong, I did appreciate sleep but as of this day I have a deeper appreciation of sleeping in the arms of God with a mind of peace.

I had an appointment this day and my mother was taking me to it. We got to the stoplight and I leaped out of the car. I figured if I was going to allow these thoughts to be at the front then I needed to act on them. I should have recognized then that there was something I needed to do on this earth because I only fell. I was hot! I mean, I seriously began to cry and asked God why He spared my life. *Why did You allow me to fall and the car to switch lanes? Are You serious? I know what I am doing. Why did You stop me?* I asked all these questions to my counselor and even to my confidant. Both had similar replies. They said that there is something that only I can do and God will make sure only you do it.

What in the world could I do? How could God use me? I had slipped into the ditch of gambling, promiscuity, debt, cursing and living a life where I wanted to be liked, loved and appreciated all because I was listening fervently to the wrong voices. I knew every song that could be sung to get me through the day, along with all the "famous" scriptures (as I like to call them), but I did not know how to apply them. I did not feel worthy to even be one of God's refined and important daughters. You know that saying, "What does not kill you will make you stronger." Well I am here to tell you; yes it will.

After I left my therapist's office I came home and sat in the dark for three whole days. I only moved to go to the bathroom and to get water. Now, I am not going to lie, when I finally moved and actually got up to get myself together, I weighed myself and saw that no weight had been lost. Honey, I got angry and that spiked a determination like never before. Let me clarify... I was determined to lose weight; you know, next year. I was now more determined to begin to practice what I had heard and seen so many others do. I placed my faith in God and begin to put it to work.

I got up on the fourth day and took what I now know was the longest shower ever. You know what happens when you are in chlorine for too long and your skin begins to look different? Let's just say when I got in the shower the sun was coming up and when I got out of the shower the sun was sitting way up in the sky and it was traffic time.

As I began to place lotion on my body, I got up and looked in the mirror and began to cry. Come on, I know there have been a lot of tears that were shed but I believe that tears do two things: they cleanse your soul and mind and they help you to see a little bit better. Now just hang in there with me, we are going to need each other for this part of the hill because we are almost to the top. As the elders say, "Press on baby, press on!" As the tears fell, the words that followed were life-changing. I recall reciting a small prayer that I heard my mother say once while at one of my many hospital stays, "Let Your words be my strength Lord God. Let Your words be my guide to keep me from falling. I need You to keep me from falling." Those words were recited so much, I believe the birds got a melody and began to sing it.

Later, I found myself on the floor. I was not on the floor looking for something; instead I was on the floor praying. It started out with me praying the 23rd Psalm, then it became personal. I confessed every worry, every fear and asked to see myself the way God Himself sees me. I asked God to place me with the right people that will help me to be accountable and consistent in my walk with Him. Are you hanging in there? There are only a few more steps and we will be at the top.

The following day I picked up the phone and called one of my sisters. I informed her about what happened and I asked her, "What do I do now?" She said, "From now on, every time you hear a thought that is from your yesterday just say 'Lord Jesus.' Every time you have an urge to go back to behaviors that you know you should not be doing, just say 'Lord Jesus.' If you have to say it 20 times in 30 minutes or 30 times in 60 minutes, say it until the thought or desire leaves. Once it leaves, then say, "Thank you Lord." No words followed after she said that because then she prayed with me. Later in that month I was preparing for once again another surgery.

This was not just any old procedure. God fixed it so this would be the last time that my head would be bothered, shaved and opened. My doctor informed me that there as a doctor at UCLA who had heard about my diagnosis and was confident that if he did this last surgery I would be okay and able to function. My mother and I discussed it with the assigned surgeon and received prayer from our pastor. It was only when I got down on my knees in my apartment that I felt a great relief and weight fall from me. Now if only the weight loss would show a little bit more, but keep praying. I will get there.

I prayed and asked God if this was the proper surgeon for this needed procedure, please give me a sign and I will go forward without questioning Your provision. The phone rang the next morning. It was my doctor excited with all of the information needed because I had been approved for the procedure. I was not sure who was excited the most—me or my mother. We were both overjoyed! I could honestly say that this time I was grateful; my being grateful was not only because of the surgery but because this was my confirmation that God had heard me. Once again, thoughts began to cross my mind and they did just that—crossed on one side and exited on the other.

It was in 2012 that the mask of **Depression** and it's wonderful partner, **Suicidal Thoughts** was removed. For the first time in a long time I was able to look at me and smile. I was finally on the road to loving what I saw looking back at me.

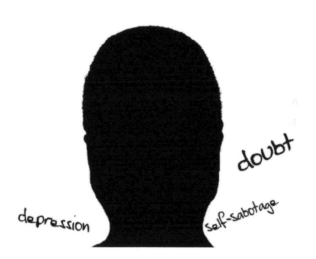

Chapter 5

My Life is Changed

My shunt had now been placed and my head was not swollen like it would be normally. Instead. I had a smile on my face. What was first explained as a condition that would have rendered me unable to do some, if not all things I did before, had been used to allow me to be better. Now, when you take this next step, you will be able to look out and see why I had to take this look back. Come on, just two more steps and we are there... the peak of joy, love, peace and grace awaits us. Ready? One and two. As I normally say when giving God praise, "Excuse me but this here requires a praise break!"

I looked out and saw all of the different roads with self-made roadblocks along with the temptations that once had me. I came out of that pit to get to the top of this hill only to prepare to go higher and higher with my Daddy, Lover and Friend. It is so much prettier at the top of this hill. Let's walk around and go the other side of it. Do not forget your water.

The shunt procedure was more than needed, it was assigned. I say that because after that surgery I have been smiling more and more and I have been listening to the right voices. The surgeon who performed the surgery was very patient and wanted to make sure that I had clarity of all that was about to happen. He came by my room the day before and asked my mother to step out. Usually I would have been nervous but this time I was collected and ready to listen.

He looked at me and asked me one question, "Do you believe in God?" I was shocked! What? Another doctor who believes in God too? This had to a "setup" as I like to say, because when God is in control, you will be set up to go up. I'll come back to that before we split up. The answer I gave him was "Yes I do!" He then said, "Good. Pray that I know what I am doing!" Wait a minute... excuse me? He then took my hand and stated that I was his assignment and he would not fail because he himself had prayed about it while he read over my entire case. The tears just flowed and flowed, so you know mommy came back into the room. She proceeded like any other mother who hears their adult baby crying. Before she could even ask, the doctor got up and said to her, "All is well. We have an understanding and she is ready. Mother, you just continue to pray." I looked at my mother and then said, "I am ready, mommy."

After the doctor left and mom and I had dinner, she went on her regular walk of the hospital. I sat up and looked out the window to see yet again, the light. It felt very familiar, but this time it had a bright look to it. It looked like a spotlight but it had a glow. I chuckled because I knew it was my Daddy, God letting me know that I can only go up from here and that everything would be alright. I fell asleep only to awaken to my mother yet again singing her song, "Let your words be my strength Lord God. Let your words be my guide..." There was a difference this time. As she sang, I began to sing along and I felt the atmosphere change.

Soon after that moment, we prayed like we always did, but it was different. This time I said I need to pray. As I prayed, I felt more and more safe, secure and ready. By that time the nurses and surgery crew had come to my room to take me down for surgery. I looked at mommy and smiled. She took my hand and said, "This time it is truly you and God."

We got down to the operating room and the feeling was nothing but peace. I was at peace because I knew that God had set this whole procedure up. All I wanted and needed to do was transfer to the table and prepare for my usual sleep.

Another highlight happened when the doctor said that he wanted to pray before we proceeded. I was more than comfortable. As a matter of fact, the first twelve minutes I was somewhat coherent just so they could make sure I was aware of what was going to happen and why I would have certain scars. I remember giving them the thumbs up and was ready to go. When that procedure was over, I was told by my mother that I awakened with a smile. I laughed and said to her, "I was playing with the angels and having a great time."

I stayed in the hospital for the shortest period ever. I was there for four days. Now you know I was more than happy, I was amazed and ready to return to Las Vegas just to begin to live for real this time. I had to go away to realize what the infamous saying that I often find myself saying even today, "Unless you can walk a mile in my shoes, go for it." However, if you cannot, I suggest you allow me to exchange my shoes. For what? Yep, a bottle of water.

Now that I was back in Las Vegas and my MRIs, CAT scans and all other tests were coming back negative, I smiled almost all the time. I was getting up in the morning and getting excited because I was beginning to feel normal. It still amazes me to this day how I am able to remember the ups and downs of this entire of journey but I am not able to remember the things that I felt I needed to. We will come back to that because once again that is a God thing and when He orchestrates something in you, it is all in order.

I was living in my own apartment. I went back to work and was preparing to begin my graduate program. I was all excited but then I made a huge mistake. Yes, it was a mistake. I now know this is not being arrogant, I just had to learn and realize that I do not and will not ever share EVERYTHING with just anyone.

If you do not get but a few things from this look back at how good God is, get this; when there is something that God wants to birth in you and have you be the steward over, your circle will change. You may often feel like you are alone, isolated or just plain forgotten about. That is not the case at all, He just needs to place all the proper people around you and remove those whose time is up. You know they say friendships last forever, well some may, but my favorite book and chapter in the Bible reminds me that to everything there is a time and season. In simple terms, we may start out together but the finish is not up to us at all.

I have always been in awe of the way God allows things to connect. A friendship reminds me of a cake. You need to make sure that you have all the ingredients so the cake will actually rise and not just be flat. That is the same thing in life and relationships. The Bible states so many things about the importance of being equal. I did not understand that until I got to this one particular part of the journey.

Remember how I told you that I was back in my own apartment and shared a bit too much information? It was on that particular day that I allowed my flesh to slip and get me into a lustful situation. Yes, I said lustful. I wanted to feed my flesh and satisfy the desire I needed. I allowed a man in my life who looked the part and spoke the part, but the mistake I made came after giving him the wrong part. I did not realize then but now I know for sure, whenever you sleep with someone you become intertwined with that person and it is only God who can deliver you from the attachment.

The one thing I need to make clear before we go any further; the masks that I spoke of before were removed for that season but one was picked right back up. **Depression** is a mask that can really take you through. It will even cause you to over-invest in items that you really do not need but you want because they will allow you to paint the face you really want. Remember when I awakened from a coma and asked if my lipstick was on? You understand now, right? Another reason why depression can last so long or be put back on is because there is something that you need to do yourself. Forgive and give it all to God!

Yes, that is something that is easier said than done but there will come a time that you get tired of applying the concealer to cover up the traces of the tears. You get tired of applying the foundation that you thought would keep you only to find out that the foundation you really need does not need to be applied, you need to make sure your house is built on it.

There will also come a time when you realize that the only thing that you must put on daily is the shield of faith, carry the sword of the Spirit and the breastplate of righteousness. I know you know what that is, right? Oh yes, you do! Even when you did not know it, you had someone praying for you and asking God to cover you with the full armor of God.

Thinking about that alone gets me ready to enter in or for the next generation and turn up for Jesus.

Just the thought of it makes me want to run! I should run anyway because that will help me get my 10,000 steps in. Look at God! He always has a plan and reward somewhere.

I knew that what I wanted was wrong ,but I was still holding a grudge of anger and had an attitude that was not willing to forgive someone in my life. I was looking for love in the places that seemed comfortable only because the man would say words to me that I never heard from my father. I could go ahead and blame my now deceased father for all of my actions but the reality is that I knew what I was doing. See, this is where I abused the free will that God gives us.

It was not until my father called me before he died and confessed all the things that he had done to me that I was able to forgive him and I asked him to forgive me. I asked him to forgive me because I had held the grudge for so long that I did block the possibility of him and me ever having a father-daughter relationship. Let me also explain this side of forgiveness that is not always spoken of; you must forgive yourself as well.

I had forgiven my father but I was angry with me. I again chose to go searching time and time again for the wrong type of love. Many say that love does not cost anything but I have a different view on that. Love was paid with the greatest price ever known by man, God sent His Son to die and take away the sins of the world. I had the audacity to slap Him in the

71

face with making willful and wrong decisions because of another part of my past. Not only was that wrong, it was an unnecessary ride. I straddled the fence. It was at that point that I began to understand what the elders said, "Either you love God and you are going to do as He asks, or you are going to live your life in the dark." I knew that I had to make a decision. I should have already made it. but you will never know a pot is hot until you touch it for yourself.

What really amazed me was that after I had done all of the "improper" things, God was still keeping me. I was taking my courses in my first graduate program, doing well and able to hold a job. I could not believe that I was still covered. I mean, I had really done some dumb things and had some crazy thoughts, but God kept me and made sure I always had shelter, food and I was in my right mind. How could this be? Why did He want to keep me from harm and danger? Why did He keep His arms of protection around me? Was this now the moment that I had read about, heard about, and what my angels had prayed for? Yes, it was. This was the point where I had to make the ultimate decision; either apply my faith and walk in it or continue in the dark.

It is pretty evident today what path I chose. Now wait before you get too happy... Let me just remind you that every single day with God is not always bright, crisp and clean. I mean, the mornings are.

Even when there is rain, like a songwriter wrote, "God has not promised us sunshine but a little rain mixed with God's sunshine." That is the type of God we serve and love. When faith is all you have, faith is all you will ever need.

This is why I know for sure that it was not my mama's faith that has allowed me to make it this far. I am truly in the arms of God and trusting Him each and every day. As I often say, with God any and everything is possible. Now if you do not give Him a praise, you know I will! Once again, pass the water for this is the final curve that we are coming up on and we must stay refreshed and hydrated. It sounded good, so I said it.

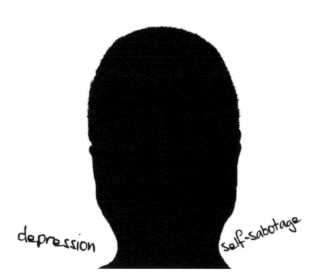

Chapter 6

God's Miraculous
Marvelous Miracle

This is the final curve of this journey. This is where I get to define the miraculous marvelous miracle. Being that life and death is in the power of the tongue, I have found myself really thinking more before I speak and asking God if something is okay or how should I handle a situation. Whenever God has stepped in or blocked anything, it was a miracle.

There were many more surgeries that I have experienced since the shunt placement. I know it sounds interesting to say; but it was always a setup. There was one in particular that really shocked us all. You know me... Whenever I hear of an event at my favorite makeup counter, I go there. As usual, I went and got in trouble buying lipstick, but I was cute. After the makeover, I experienced a great deal of pain. My stomach was tightening up and I had to crawl from the restroom to the valet in order for me to get home. Once I got home, I laid out on the floor and just moaned and began to regurgitate.

I could not take this pain at all. I knew I had to call the ambulance, but you know me! It may appear vain, but all of the doctors on my medical team know that I shall always arrive nicely. So I crawled around my home and made sure I had everything I needed. Once this was done and the ambulance was called, the process of what I now call "the removal of all things" blocking. You will understand what I mean once I continue to explain.

Once I arrived to the first hospital, the regurgitation kept going for 23 hours. Yes, one hour short of a complete day. I felt like three days had passed but it was just 23 hours. I had taken so many x-rays and had been given so much medicine that I found myself yearning for morphine. This was a narcotic that I was already used to. Since I had begun my medicinal journey so many years before, my body had become immune to it. Let me just pause here for a moment. I will admit that I liked morphine because it is a strong medicine. You must be monitored, but I had nice file at almost all of the hospitals. I began to ask for the amount and they just proceeded to supply it.

After the last dose of morphine, I was transferred to another hospital where the procedure was done. It was an emergency because the doctor had seen the x-rays and was worried that there was too much damage done. If that procedure was not done, I would not be here today.

After I was transported and had a brief free moment from the regurgitation, I asked the nurse if I was still glowing from my makeover. She replied, "I have never seen a patient so beautiful." I was happy about that, but my stomach was not. Before the surgery began, my God-given grandma prayed with me and told me that this was just a part of my testimony.

We went into the operating room and my favorite doctor had arrived; the anesthesiologist. He and I were talking and he explained what was going to happen. Then he read my file and said, I think you know already what is going to happen. I agreed and smiled because he too said that I was the prettiest patient he had worked with in a while; I guess the word got around that I would cooperate with a little bit of flattery. I was relaxed now and ready for the procedure to begin.

When I finally awakened from the anesthesia, I found myself with tubes in my nose but I did not feel them because I was given my favorite medicine once again. My mother and my cousin were in my room when I awakened and they were all smiling. Now I know you know what I asked, right? "Is my lipstick on?" All of us laughed—well they did. I could only hit my hand on the bed. I was happier this time after surgery because I knew that I would not be embarrassed to handle my food and drinks at all. I was also excited because there would not be any form of therapy happening after this procedure. Instead I would be able to share my story with you and encourage you.

That was the last curve of the look back and we have come to the top of the mountain. The view is amazing! There was a time when I would have looked out at this view and just shook my head. Now that God is in total control and you have looked back with me, I know that there is nothing that I cannot do. As we look out at this view, I am able to see my life in a better light and find a simple melody and the harmony of it all. I am saying that being up here is not easy—by any means it is not—but when you are able to look to hills from where your help and strength come from, you to know that this too shall pass. I often find myself looking at my journals and reading all the hurt and anger that I was full of and then smiling because only God could remove that and make me smile.

Since the final surgery I have had some other medicinal encounters that I will have to deal with forever according to my doctors, but we both know Who the greatest doctor is, so I am not worried. I look at my encounters or seizures as moments to shake things off. I know that I can be one of God's most stubborn daughters and need to get reeled in. God knows exactly how to get my attention.

I have been blessed to have great mentors and angels as I have approached this beautiful peak, but the one thing that I will say is that the people who began with me are not present. I will admit that I questioned God about it many, many times. One of my mentors reminded me that everyone cannot go with me everywhere. I knew that was true and it had to happened, but I still did not get it. As usual, I found myself caring a little bit too much. I began to call and see how people were doing. I know having a big heart is a good thing, but even those of us with big hearts need to have it covered and resting in the arms of God.

Since I now knew that and had finally understood the importance of release and a time for everything, I decided to just pray and give it all to God. I have encountered some of those people I like to call "expired folks," and when I see them I find myself in awe at my own behavior. I remember when I would question someone as to why we were not speaking anymore. Instead, I give them a hug and still say I love you.

It may sound funny or even weird because as I began to do it more often, I thought the same thing. Thankfully, there is power in forgiveness. Forgiveness is a like a coin; it has two sides. Let's look at this together. The side with heads is normally the person who has done the damage, caused the pain or said some words that really did not need to be uttered. The tails side is the side of you and me. It is on this side that we must apply the fruits of the Spirit.

Let's just be honest with each other. How many times have you landed on tails and tried to flip it back to heads just for the other person to really understand that they need to be careful of what they are saying and be careful of what could happen next? I will be honest with you. There have been times when I did not even flip a coin; I just gave a response and then it would go to another level that neither one of us needed to go.

It became even more difficult for me to ask for assistance because my **PRIDE** began to show its face. Was this all because I did not want to forgive? You may be asking, "How does this tie into pride?" When a person allows their pride to show, they begin to think that something is owed to them because they were offended. Now, this is what I experienced, so I am not trying to step on anyone's toes or call anyone out, but if I am going to encourage someone I must be honest and transparent.

As a result of allowing pride to rule and reign, I would always have confrontations. Most of the time they were small, microscopic, or flat out over nothing. See what I mean? Reaching this peak does not mean it is going to now be easy, it just means that I am more accountable and able to pick and choose which battles I will fight, or shall I say "assist" God with. I will come back to picking and choosing but let me continue to explain the importance of **Forgiveness**.

Now that I had used every negative word and had participated in too many confrontations, I found myself isolated in a way. I was with my mother and some friends, but the friends that I felt were important were not speaking to me. Yes, I was mad and said to myself, "It is not me, it is them."

One day at my usual spot in the mall, I saw someone that I had a confrontation with and we actually hugged each other. We sat down and had some tea and cookies. She looked at me and said I need to say something to you and if you do not accept it, it is okay, but in order for me to move forward I must make this wrong right. She began to explain how her life had changed and how she was now on a road of peace. She went on to ask if I would forgive her for her words and actions. I looked at her with a face full of questions and asked her to explain why she was asking for my forgiveness. Now, do not get confused; I did not ask the question as if I were due this explanation. You know how we must get an understanding in all things. I was seeking some understanding. She looked at me and laughed. She shared that she too had to ask her spiritual mother why must this be done. She told me that a lack of forgiveness is not any of the fruits of the Spirit and if you are to use that infamous question, "What would Jesus do?" then you should be willing to apply the fruit of love and add a shot of forgiveness.

We both sat there and laughed. I then asked her if she would forgive me for reacting and not thinking. She said, "I have already forgiven you but I suggest that if there is anyone that you need to forgive, you may want to do so, so that you can continue to grow and unblock your blessings."

Why is it that in order for the blessings to come, appear or simply be revealed, we forget that we too must do some work? I remember all of the sermons and the conversations, but I will admit that majority of the time I only focused on what God would do and what His Word said. Often, I just read the scripture alone—not the one or two above it or after it. I just focused on the easy part or what I thought was easy. The only thing that was easy, was the realization that although the situation involved me, I really had nothing to say at all.

I can hear my elders in my head repeating to me, "Baby, a lie is something that you never have to defend, just give to Jesus and make sure they do not leave your thirsty or hungry." I can laugh at that today simply because I finally understand what they were speaking of and why it was so important to give them water and/or food before they departed. I love my elders and appreciate all the wisdom given, even if it took me a few minutes to understand it all.

Remember how I said that I would explain the desire to assist God with my battle? Yes, I even laugh as I am reflecting upon this part of the journey. I know that God is good all by Himself and does not need my assistance at all—just my faith. I had to get to the top of this mountain to realize that. I have to admit that I often think that when God hears me talking to Him or about Him, He listens with a look that only a parent can give to their child because the love they have for them surpasses all that they have done and will do.

Knowing that God is all-powerful and has all things in control should be enough for me many times, but because I am flesh and I want results now, I often stepped in the middle when God Himself had better and more efficient plan.

I just needed to apply faith and that p-word I have come to appreciate on many levels, **Patience.** I hope you have noticed by now that I stopped praying for patience a long time ago and began asking for strength because with strength comes patience. Please get that or listen when someone shares a story about patience. The reality is that you may admire Job and his story, but that is it, admire it. Leave the rest of it between Job and the Lord. Now do not get me wrong, making it to the top of the mountain does not mean that it will be a smooth road from this point on; no way. As a matter of fact, the road has gotten to be a bit narrower and not as many rest stops along the way.

Let me expound on how the road became narrower. It got tight for a moment because I found myself going backwards. Instead of me taking the time to do what was asked of me to do, I was doing what I believed I needed to do. You and I have become friends because of the sharing of this journey, but due to the thoughts of my past being repeated in my mind and shown in my actions, I traveled back to the place of discomfort to find some comfort for the moment. I went to the clubs, had drinks, made temporary friends, popped pills and again returned to sleeping with the enemy. Now that I am looking back, I have to lift up my hands. As I lift them up, I chuckle at the fact of knowing that even when I did not want to be kept and receive real love, God still kept a hedge of protection around me.

Truthfully, I will admit that there have still been moments even at the top of this peak where I am able to look out and see how far God has brought me and where I am going. Even so, that I still put on the mask of **Low Self-Esteem.** I found that whenever I began to sit and look at other people and the things that they had or the people that were in their lives, I would apply the mask. I would only take it off once I return to the stillness of my home. Even there I would make sure all the doors were locked and then go into my bedroom and remove the mask in its totality.

I am happy to say that the journey of writing this book and becoming transparent has allowed me to fully understand Whose I am, who I am in God and see myself the way God sees me. Yes, it has taken all of that, along with the talks from just a few of His assigned best to get me to this place where I am content.

He has allowed me to understand exactly what having faith really means. It is not just the substance of things hoped for and the evidence of things not seen but it is a lifestyle. I have come to a place where I am no longer fearful of being alone for I am not lonely. This will made me laugh when I realized it but I am now at a place where I actually count before I respond. I laughed at that when I first did it because there were words that ran across my mind to say but all that would come out was, "One, two, three, four, five..." and "Wait, what did you say?"

I have come to a place of peace when topics are discussed and issues are brought to the forefront. I can discuss rape and molestation without actually doing it again to myself. I am able now to rejoice with people instead of being envious of them. I did not and am not trying to walk on any path that they have had to walk to get to where they are.

I am able to fully understand that there is a time and season for everything on this earth and in this life. I have a better outlook and greater appreciation for the simplicity of life. I am aware that not everyone who smiles with you on Sunday will or should remain with you on Monday. I am no longer living to please and be liked by others, no; I am living to make sure that I am present and accounted for at the second fish fry.

I have come to hold myself accountable for all the things I say, do and how I act. I have come full circle on so many things that I often sit at my desk and listen to the loud roar of the stillness. It helps me to understand that I have a purpose according to God's plan, timing, direction and protection. I will always see myself as one of God's Miraculous Marvelous Miracles. This look back has allowed me to appreciate the foundation that was laid for me at the beginning, for truly it was NOT MY MAMA'S FAITH.

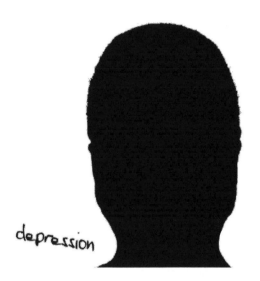

Chapter 7

Simplicity in Words

These are just some words that I have written (on social media and in my quiet time) that I thought were just for me to encourage myself; however they may also encourage you too. Be encouraged as you strive towards your destiny. Love you!!

Just Saying Thank You

"God You are everything I need and more. I thank You for being my constant. Thank You for making all things new and keeping it simple. I am right at the threshold of my destiny and I know that the devil is mad, but I continue to praise You and worship You through it all.

Every time I have a ache or my shunt shifts, I will continue to give You praise. Every time I have a seizure and I come out of it, I will still give You praise. I thank you Lord for keeping me on this journey. I will forever give You praise! My life is truly a testimony and You are more than worthy of all the glory and honor. In Jesus name, I thank You for fighting this fight with me. I serve you notice devil, if all you have is seizures and headaches, you have the wrong one! GOD IS A HEALER AND RESTORER OF LIFE... Next..."

People have always said when life gives you lemons make lemonade. That may be true, but you know I like to add my own little kick to things...

I say when life hands you lemons, ask for sugar, ice and maybe some rum.

Then add to it all that you want and make it fun.

You make life your own and have your own beat

Because really the only person keeping up with it is you and your two feet

Make life what God says it should be, not what he said or she said

Or what society thinks

So when life hands you lemons, make a cake or a stiff drink

The only choice that is really valid is the one that you pick and distinct

Side Note: The poem above was written with little effort but with great feeling and emotion. It is in the moments of awe like this that I am able to get a clear understanding of how much God loves me and trusts me. I know that God will get all the glory out of this because someone's life will be changed and made brand new forever.

My Being

I am almost close

I can see the finish line

I am not going to look behind

I am going to press, press toward the finish line

I am going to stretch my hands to the only Help I know

I am going to hold Your hand as you miraculously work Your plan

I am ready this time; to walk and follow You

I am ready to respond to the things You say, for that I must truly trust and obey

I knew I should've been with You from the start but You knew then that I was not ready to give You my heart

I thank You Lord for being all I need; my mother, my Father, my lover

Simply everything

I am glad that it is in You I have my BEING!

Open Window

The sky is open

Crystal clear to be exact

No cloud to be found, wind at my back

As I look up and see only the sun

The shine of it, its sparkle and glow

The essence of its presence

I wonder if the sun knows it's worth and its need

The need to be seen

The need to be gleaned in

The need to give plants a reason to stand

The need to give grass a want to grow,

Wait

The sun is now moving, it must be a wink

Ha, ha, ha

No, that's just my Daddy showing He hears me and He's pleased.

The Haircut

I was sitting in the chair waiting for what I thought would be just another haircut. Snip here, snip there and a twist and a turn and I would be done. However when the clippers were in use a whole different experience began.

As the clippers moved in closely burdens were lifted. Doubt, fear, worry and insecurities that I once allowed to block me from my destiny were now clipped, snipped, and faded away. All edges were on the floor. Now I have a greater appreciation for what haircuts are for....

BREAKING NEWS:

What God has for me is for me. It may be delayed but it is not denied. You may think I do not deserve it, but remember the devil is and will forever will be a lie. So instead of trying to figure out why I am so blessed and still in the race, seek His face and ask God for His grace, mercy and favor to pass all the tests that you have yet to face. Would you like some water as you continue to run your assigned race?

Made in the USA
Lexington, KY
27 October 2019